On Work

an anthology

On Work

Published by Unleash Press

Reynoldsburg, OH 43068

unleashcreatives.net/press

Book Cover by Christopher Shanahan

Edited by Jen Knox

Printed in the United States of America

ISBN 979-8-9862743-7-9

An Anthology

Contents

POETRY

PROSE

Dr. Deidra Suwanee Dees

Dr. Deidra Suwanee Dees' family descend from Hotvlkvlke (Wind Clan) following Muscogee stompdance traditions. She serves as Director/Tribal Archivist at the Poarch Band of Creek Indians. She teaches Native American Studies at University of South Alabama, tribally sponsored. For the past twelve years, she has been a contributing writer to the *Poarch Creek News*, retitled, *Creek Corner Magazine*. Her poetry manuscript titled, *Indian Ice: Indigenous Witness*, is forthcoming from Get Fresh Books Publishing.

2023 Editors' Choice Winner

Excerpts from *Indian Ice: Indigenous Witness / Estv-Cate' Het'ute*

I. Childhood Work
Sweat

I feel the sweat watering my forehead,
dripping below my brows in the middle of
acres of tall cotton stalks.

I am smothered, bending over, searching for
cotton near the ground
as gnats and salt blur my vision.

Dirty sweat runs down my legs, making me
vulnerable to mosquitoes hiding
in the shade of the cotton leaves, while

the scorching hot sun presses the back of
my head, like heavy mountains of granite.

The repulsive smell of my own body odor
crowds my nostrils as I squat
between the rows, gasping in the heat,

seeing a sea of brown-skinned faces
dotting the white cotton field
while other kids sit in the shade of the house, which
makes me hate my body—*I hate myself.*

II. College Work
Hard Labor

stretched-out path from the
        cotton fields of Alabama,

hard labor from my intellect, not my body,
inside the concrete and steel of Boston
        supports my household
        as I study to become a teacher,

flashbacks of childhood
invade me,
        bent over in my high-rise with
        dirt-colored carpet,

I pick up tufts of cotton
pulled from my puppy's fuzzy turtle toy

III. Career Work
Speeding

speeding around the car
in front of me,

weaving my way from the
rez to campus

to teach Indigenous
Studies,

skinny two-
lane,

like playing checkers with
Daddy,

I jump one
at a time, until I am king

Teaching

almost   to campus

teaching
        Introduction

to Indigenous Studies,

windows down, a
student in John Deere green
        dump truck

in front of me

bumping to the rhythm
of
        "Redneck Woman"

as we
slow down at the light

IV. Self Work
What Will I Wear?

Do I want to go suit and tie?
So many skirts, so many colors; or, do I want to
go casual today?
earrings of quill? And what about
that special
chinaberry necklace?

Hurriedly,
stopping by the Smoke Shop
for gasoline and breakfast,
I encounter a White man with unbrushed teeth.
Mind faded along with his collar,
perhaps once starched.
If I could see through the grit,
I could tell.
His jeans are tattered,
his jacket doesn't match, and
his hat has expired above.
his thin, unbathed body.

On Work

COVID has not taken
my job at the college, but perhaps it
took his. Why do I have the luxury of choosing
what I want to wear,
while this man wears daily his few possessions?
Holding out my sandwich and
Marlboros,
I hand him breakfast.
An embarrassed, humbled thank you pushes
through his crusted lips.

He admires me!
I do next to nothing for him,
and he admires me.
As I drive off watching him in my rearview,
he stands there, admiring me;
how could he admire me when
I have passed him by
on that same way to work
days upon days—days without number?

An Anthology

Willa Schneberg

Willa Schneberg is a poet, essayist, visual artist, curator and psychotherapist in private practice. She has authored five poetry collections including: *In The Margins of The World*, recipient of the Oregon Book Award; *Storytelling in Cambodia*, and *Rending the Garment*. She has been a fellow at Yaddo and MacDowell. Work has appeared in numerous anthologies and literary journals, including *American Poetry Review; Salmagundi; Poet Lore; Bellevue Literary Review, Calyx: A Journal of Art and Literature by Women,* and *The Journal of Psychohistory. The Naked Room* will be out from Broadstone Books in 2023.

Confidentiality

You carry their angst with you—
a basket filled with quivering raw eggs.
Clients must never know your fear of cracking.
You must embody what they barely tell themselves:

they are the man who shaves the right side of his face first,
instead of the left (for him that's the improper order),
and must scrape the left side again until it bleeds;

the woman who cries diabetes makes her husband slur
and unsteady as a drunk,
but refuses to be his nursemaid,

the young man who says he "understands"
why his girlfriend likes girls, so does he,
but since the threesome, he fears
she might really like girls more;

the wife of the sex-addict who hates
all the women in his computer,
and the whores, not virtual, and prays
her breast implants will win him back;

the senior who finally accepts his marriage is over,
although he rescued his much younger
wife from a cult, and now believes
he was no hero, just another master;

On Work

The mother who doesn't want her college age son
to move back if he smokes pot. This week, no talk
of her alcoholic paramour, "who has got to go."

Today, one exits, one walks in. The 2 o'clock
will never know the grief of the client before her,
whose twin embryos clotted out of her body,

and the 1 o'clock won't feel even worse, not knowing
that the 2 o'clock, who never wanted children, is elated
since her abortion went without a hitch.

For you, it's like holding a dragonfly by its wings
trying not to tear them off.

Dream Session, Client I

The panes in my apartment are small, don't open,
and there is a refrigerator with a cubbyhole
wide enough for the DSM and a spigot for tears.

You find the matzo and the jar of peanut butter,
help yourself, and say, *You probably have*
another favorite client now.

"I spy you floating around outside my office suite.
You never wear muumuus. Stop it, stop
knocking on every door but mine.
After so many years together you owe me
a finale and applause, but instead you jump ship."

You just couldn't, you say. *Sorry.*
Please accept this dream good-bye.
With you I almost erased my mother.
If I ever turn myself inside out again
it won't be with you.

You rub the crumbs off your mouth:
Who knows? Without you
I might do the same old same old, and
pick up men whose fists shut me up
force me to change locks.

Dream Session, Client II

I walk down a spindly railed staircase
from my private life to an unfinished basement
crammed with giant white plastic bags
filled with client files.

You stand at the foot of the stairs:

> *This could be a one-shot deal.*
> *I thought I would show up*
> *for my regular appointment*
> *to see if you had filled it.*
>
> *My parents are almost eighty now,*
> *and I still don't love them. I acquiesced*
> *to be with them in London.*
>
> *At the Tower we watched the Beefeaters*
> *march stiffly into place.*
> *I couldn't wait to get away.*

I am dreaming, so I can self-disclose
visiting the Big Apple, and not telling my parents
I was down the street, and divulge

that although my mother said "that when you were young
you loved your father best," I don't remember
ever loving him.

Pearls

I wish I could have been with you
and Dr. Orne* in his office, you both sucking
in cigarette smoke, letting it curl out
through your nostrils, when you said,

I want to be the child not the mother.
It should be innate, why have I failed so miserably?

My words on paper spark, don't you think??

You thought writing might be good for me.
These runes are really yours too.

I would have seen you twist
the string of pearls around your neck
until it burst open, pearls cascading.

One by one, I would have picked them up,
to place them in your cupped hands—
all that milky light,

and say, "Your poems are your pearls,
yours alone."

**Dr. Martin T. Orne was Anne Sexton's psychiatrist.*

Katherine Edgren

Katherine Edgren's latest book, *Keeping Out the Noise*, is scheduled to be published by Kelsay Books in 2022. In addition to her book The Grain Beneath the Gloss, published by Finishing Line Press, she also has two chapbooks: Long Division and Transports and has been published in numerous journals including: *Coe Review, Third Wednesday, Christian Science Monitor, Birmingham Poetry Review, Peninsula Poets, the Decadent Review, Light, Orchards Poetry Journal,* and *Barbaric Yawp,* among others. She has a Master's Degree in Social Work from the University of Michigan, and lives in Dexter, Michigan.

Country Club

Ambrose arose in his knife-creased pants, clean white jacket,
linen napkin draped on his arm, and led patrons
to flower-decked tables or the bar.
An elderly black man, *ninety*—they said.
Quiet, with the sweetest smile, the loveliest name.
Ambrose, immortal.

A friend to everyone: from the Bookkeeper I assisted every day
after school, to the industrious ladies who diced and pounded
and cooked the food, and scrubbed pots and pans in the kitchen
with their strong hands. This community of larks sang
as they flour-dusted the chickens or mashed the potatoes—
about their daughters, their bus rides to work, their men.
I chatted with them during breaks, or on the way to the powder room.
One had been a masseuse, and a few times used her kneading skills
on my back. Ebullient Lucille, the Head Cook, used to shriek:
"Ooh, I love to hear myself scream!"

Their muffled words and abandoned laughter
would drift under the door that separated their kitchen
from my dark cave of an office lit by one florescent bulb,
where I totaled up bar and food bills collected by Ambrose
until the numbers matched—
watching signatures deteriorate with every drink.
I stapled the adding machine tapes onto the stacks of bills

On Work

where they dragged like sorry tails

and handed over these productions to my boss: the Bookkeeper.
Her white legs were encased in sheer white nylons.
She sported a tight round ball of hair high on the back of her head,
wore tailored suits and dresses—
and carried tight little buns at the base of her spine.

One day she told me if I liked my job,
I shouldn't fraternize with "the help,"
          as though we weren't.

Coroner's Office, Memphis, 1972

Every afternoon, I'd steel myself
before shuffling through the Polaroid stack
left on my desk corner for filing:
dead bodies from the day before. Evil rashes
of shotgun wounds, the surprised eyes of those
who knew they were goners glaring back at me.
Drownings—bodies puffed up like small whales,
suicides by gun to mouth or head.
I am still haunted by the wild eyes
of the speed addict who OD'd in the closet,
and by the thick, Ascaris worms crawling out
of the orifices of children as they cooled—
children who had played in a parasite-laced sandbox
in this city of neglect and despair.

John Davis

John Davis is a polio survivor and the author of *Gigs* and *The Reservist*. His work has appeared recently in *DMQ Review, Iron Horse Literary Review* and *Terrain.org*. He lives on an island in the Salish Sea.

Instructions for Night Watch

Know the privacy of this guard shack.
Spiders build towers as if conducting
a symphony. Trees blade the wind.
The last of the leaves flaps the glass.
Sky is painted black gauze and the space
heater hums a flurry of static.

Know the hoagie shop across the street
stuffs meatballs between whole wheat buns.
To feel the grease run down your hands,
To lick it off your thumbs. To bury your face
into red peppers, lettuce, cheese. Sesame
seeds stick between your teeth. Know it.

You're the man. Seaman Apprentice.
Shitbird the gunner's mate calls you.
Hope like hell no terrorist bashes the gate.
You only have a karate kick you learned
on TV. But you're the man. Watery and dark
in the guard shack. Night's salvation.

Sideways

It may have been 1964 in Seattle,
Vietnam heating up,
but in our house it was 1864.
Mother retold the Battle of Nashville
battle charge by battle charge
tightening her jaw and spitting *Yankee*
like a rotten prune: *Yannnkee*.
Cousin this died. Cousin that died honorably,
every man named Colonel as far as I could tell.
I should be proud to wear a uniform.
Father poured more wine and toasted
the hunters in the bird shooting prints.
With her fork, Mother snapped
my elbows on the table

the way the drill instructor snapped
at me years later.
I was such a shitbird, disgrace to my country.
Did my mother send me here to piss him off?
No wonder we weren't winning Vietnam
with a shitbird like me who had a seabag
stuffed up his ass. I didn't care
about communists in Vietnam as I elbowed
my way across the compound, sideways on all fours,
spitting out dirtballs the size of prunes,
bleeding in the heat, wondering why war
is so handsome at a dinner table.

An Anthology

Ed Woods

Ed Woods was born in Toronto and now lives in Dundas, Ontario. His writing is heavily influenced by his work and life experiences. His first published poem related to work as a crew member upon Natural Gas Pipelines and other works reflect his time as a recreation instructor, aircraft pilot, chemical tanker driver, telephone cable splicer, night shift taxi driver, and municipal snowplow operator. His most creative times seem to surface when multi-tasking such as driving a transport truck or flying an aircraft where decisions are without clutter. Ed has published several chapbooks and was a contributor to the 2022 *Conversations* anthology by Unleash Press.

Just Another Shift

Main streets get enough care,
but I drive regional.
Outskirt routes need attention,
remote of tire and footprints.

No streetlights to border.
Pines mix with assorted trees
that snake through farmland.

I turn toward a sparse area,
brake my vehicle to stop at
the scene of heartbreak with a
moonlit backdrop.

A body hangs frozen
from a steel cable line.
Frosted remnants of animation.

EMS summoned,
respectful removal,
a coroner verifies
names and family,
notifies survivors.
A horror I will never know.

As I drive, I think about the officer,
this unwanted task
No one who views a uniform
will keeps passive memory,
including the messenger.

One Million

Service call to a bank vault.
Manager handed me some Plexi-glass,
said it was my new paperweight
for home office purposes.

Two thin pieces screwed together.
I threw it in the tool case
without a glance and thought,
nowadays, it seems people avoid paper

He said to take good care of it.
I looked down, almost passed
out. A one-million-dollar bill
protected by plastic layers.

He laughed at my reaction
while I thought of what this one bill could do
Change a life and ease constraints,
or help a community,
make thousands of citizens happy

I handed it back and wondered
who could make change?
This micro-thin bill carried power
that my biweekly payroll
would never attain.

An Anthology

Julie Martin

A poet and a public-school teacher, Julie Martin lives near the confluence of the Mississippi and Minnesota Rivers. Her poetry has appeared in several online journals, most recently: *The Talking Stick*, *Plants and Poetry*, *Writers Resist*, *Mothers Always Write*, *Thimble Literary Magazine*, and *Gravitas*.

Mary Tyler Moore Joins the Union

From across Nicollet Mall, she winks at me.

Throwing the gauntlet, she hurls her tam in the air:

Love is all around, no need to fake it!

We are weaving our way through the throng.

You can have the town, why don't you take it?

Marching with thousands of educators and supporters,

gathered in front of The Government Plaza

Greta Callahan, our MFT59 president,

cries out, "We are in a fight for the soul of our city".

The bronze statue of Mary scintillates assent.

Our picket signs raised for "Safe and Stable Schools",

Mary extends her hand, picks up a sign,

beams down on us, effervescent,

dons a union blue stocking cap without mussing her flip.

You're gonna make it after all.

Larry Pike

Larry Pike lives with his wife, Carol, in Glasgow, Kentucky. His writing has been published in a variety of publications, and he was a 2021 Best of the Net nominee. Finishing Line Press published his debut poetry collection, *Even in the Slums of Providence*, in October 2021.

Money for Grad School

—found in a Twitter thread

I did some things.
Two other poets and I were the summer
landscaping crew at an assisted living facility.
In a bookstore, I filled potpourri bins, turned on

dreaded Windham music when the boss returned.
I called bingo at local bars. I wrote
role-playing scripts for an HR department,
PR for a beer coozie, blogposts on diabetic foot ulcers,

tens of thousands of words until I couldn't stand it.
I answered questions on a grammar hotline,
loaded pallets in a barbeque sauce factory,
sang in a Catholic church choir, unstacked chairs

and set up tables for Sunday brunch.
I was an international bone marrow courier.
I called alumni for money, got shorted $50
on a paycheck, then moved back in with my parents.

I did some things I shouldn't.
I stood on a scalding sidewalk dressed as a pickle
for an entire week. I bottled moonshine,
managed a porn store. I sold stuff—leather

jackets in a hotel conference room for a guy
who went town to town, tenured professors'
lunches I stole from the department fridge,
my ex's engagement ring, a gold filling. I picked up

trash at a strip club at the edge of town in the dark
because the parking lot didn't have lights.
The most legal thing I did was being a housekeeper
for a dominatrix, many of whom are grad students.

I did some things I shouldn't say here.
I was an underwear influencer, but nude
modeling I did before and still do, so I don't know
if it counts. As the TA in the academic ethics office,

I became a professional plagiarist. I was a pseudo-
patient at a med school. I endured invasive exams
while docs-to-be and instructors talked about me
like I was a cadaver, donated a little chunk of armpit,

let them shave layers of skin off my ass, obviously
a metaphor, participated in a study where I couldn't
wash one hand for two weeks. I watched toilet paper
commercials eyes open *Clockwork Orange*-style.

And I performed at the poetry brothel, late-night intimacy
through whispered poetry. Selling plasma always helped,
though my mother disapproved. I sold plasma.
That taste in your mouth. I know,

the privilege.

An Anthology

John Peter Beck

John Peter Beck was raised near Lake Michigan in Michigan's Upper Peninsula in the port town of Escanaba. He has been a labor education professor at Michigan State University for over three decades where he co-directs a program on labor history and workers culture, Our Daily Work/Our Daily Lives The attached poems are part of two series, "Nashville Cab" and "The Work of Saints." The first features cab drivers who John used when he was flying in and out of the Nashville airport. The second mines the intersection of occupations with the Catholic patron saints associated with them. His work has been published by *The Louisville Review*, *The Seattle Review*, *Passages North* and *Another Chicago Magazine*, among others.

Nashville Cab

Family Business

She's driving Daddy's cab
in the daylight – his face stares
down from the visor.
A little of each driver ages
on the visor, the dash, the seat.
Not much scenery in the car,
Dad's ID and the Mac bag
standing in breakfast salute.
Instead, she is surrounded
by her music.
The jazz pours out
strong and she cranks it up,
waiting to see if I mind.
She's not shy and it's no bother.
The Dexter Gordon tune turns
right and soars. The cab
turns left and drops me.

The Laziest Man in Nashville

He claims you'll find no man lazier,
or one with more hate for work.
I might be his last fare
or maybe one more.
He's laying out the next two days
– going fishing – hates to work.
He hands out free advice
on watering the lawn
or surviving the next war.
"It's bound to come.
Too many people and not
enough money.
It's people and economics."
He wants two big catfish.
People and economics.
He'll lay out for three days
and hit his sisters for all
the vegetables he can carry.
They never refuse him.
He's always been special.

The Work of Saints

The Cook

Still wearing my ashes,
I told my boss at the diner
I was giving up working
for lent. She told me

that was fine since
without a paycheck
I could save up
all my hunger

for Easter dinner.
That made me think
about hunger and all
the food I cleaned

off the plates
after the lunch rush.
My mother always told me
to clean my plate,

that there were starving children
somewhere in China, Africa or
anywhere but here.
I told my mom

On Work

the leftovers would spoil
by the time they got there.
Here at work, the scraps
go in the trash

where the homeless
sift and mine them.
St. Martha, when I found
the dead man behind

the dumpster, I wanted
the Lord to raise him up
like he raised your brother,
like Lazarus. You are

our diner's patron, you watch
over all of us and we thank you
for the small moments
of peace and grace between

waves of customers, the clear ring
each time we hit the bell
when a big tip
goes into the jar.

The Coffee Roaster

The roasting is done,
beyond any last gasp
of my help or hindrance.

Horribly disfigured, a test
of faith to behold,
St. Drogo lived out

his days in a tightly walled cell,
only a tiny window facing
the square and the world outside,

barely admitting scant morsels of food,
moments of drink, sunlight,
moonlight and the Eucharist.

There is no truth
in his pilgrimage, his patronage,
his parentage

of coffee – no journey
back to Europe, his sacks
saddle bound, no beans

from places far flung, exotic,
all the lands
he never travelled.

On Work

I'll have him pray
for me and my next batch
anyway. Colombian, dark

roast filling the air,
thick, rich,
comfortable

in its certainty –
like his daily litany
and liturgy of words

wafting into the air,
the aroma of faith, strongly
rising to heaven from his cup.

The Radiologist

What would I do
if the patient's x-rays
came back

with a clear image
of the soul, unassailable
evidence of the presence

of God? As it is,
any shadow, suspected
but undetectcd, is

not good news. St. Gabriel,
your clarion voice has guided us
across the testaments.

Help me -
if only my hands
could teach the machine

to erase the cancers,
heal the broken bones
and ease all fear.

The next patient
is waiting, a small boy
with his life

stretching out before him,
once he leaves
my cold, dark room.

An Anthology

Juliana Zalon

Juliana Zalon is an English teacher in Westchester, NY. When she's not teaching real-life teenagers or creating imaginary ones in her novels, she writes her observations about being a mom for the *Westchester County Mom Collective*. She was a Semi-Finalist for the Norman Mailer High School Teacher Writing Award and had a piece published in the *New York Times Metropolitan Diary*. She has degrees from The University of Michigan, Columbia University: Teachers College, and Concordia University.

Lockdown

The gray box, its concentric circles like the watchful eyes of some arachnid Big Brother, crackled to life.

"This is Principal Lin. We are going into Lockdown. This is not a drill. There's an active shooter in the building. This is not a drill. Go into Lockdown immediately—"

Stella had been refilling her water bottle at the fill-up station in a far corner of the building. The announcement had been faint, and Stella strained to hear it. She figured it was another reminder about the parking lot or midterms. When she heard "drill," she darted into the nearest classroom. The word *Lockdown* echoed through the empty room.

"Oh God," she whispered. For a moment Stella didn't move. She cocked her head, listening. For what? She wasn't sure. Gun shots? More instructions?

She touched the ID tag dangling from her neck then ran to check the hallway for students as doors banged shut. *Bathroom,* she thought.

"Anyone here?" Stella called. No one answered. A pair of white tennis shoes, the kind the cheerleaders wore, moved under the stall. A girl emerged, trembling.

"Come," Stella said, reaching for the girl's arm. They ran across the hall, and Stella took one final look before checking the lock and slamming the door behind them.

"Over there," she instructed. "Get down. By the desk." The words fired from her mouth. Quick. Clipped. The girl obeyed, her knees shaking as she sat, hugging them tightly to her chest.

On Work

Later, Stella would wish she had been gentler.

***

On the way to school that morning, Stella ran a stop sign. She took the same route each day, moving like the turtle from the early coding program she learned in elementary school. Lefts and rights and ups and downs until the turtle stopped and a star formed (or, for Stella, something kaleidoscopic; computers weren't her thing).

But today she had been thinking about her son. How she had screamed at him, her voice emerging from deep in her throat, her teeth clenched, the fury finding its place in her brows and making a permanent home. Stella sailed through the intersection, her hands gripping the wheel, as she recalled the sound of her voice that morning.

Thankfully the other car stopped, the blare of the horn loud enough to stop her mind's guilt-march. Her heart raced at the near miss, and she waved her apologies to the other driver, moving more carefully now, the moment's alternate ending taking its place in her thought parade.

***

Stella felt the steady pulse of her heart for the second time that day. The room was smaller than her classroom, and there were tables instead of desks. She briefly wondered where the teacher might be but pushed the thought away. Stella grabbed a table and shoved it towards the door, the screeching of metal against tile making her wince. She listened for a moment then lifted it the rest of the way.

She went to the window. They were on the third floor and, she estimated, about a thirty-foot drop. Stella was never a great math student, always preferring words to numbers, but she thought they could make it. If she could get the girl to jump.

When Stella would tell this story later, when she could find a way to form the words, people would ask: *Why didn't you just jump out the window?* It was the *just* that bugged her, a black fly on a sticky paper trap.

Stella looked over at the girl on the floor. She was curled up as if she could stuff herself into her body like those foldable rain jackets. Stella wanted to speak to her. To ask her name, to give her a hug. Instead she sat down, unsure of what to do.

Stella stared at the ancient intercom. She replayed Principal Lin's message in her mind, trying to recall the sound of her voice, if the administrator had sounded scared or angry or alert. Wasn't she supposed to announce the area of the building the shooter was in? Hadn't that been part of their training in September?

She wanted to ask the girl: *Did you hear what Principal Lin said? Did she say where the threat is? Do you know what's happening out there? Do you know* anything?

Stella went back to the window. It overlooked the parking lot and she had a partial view of the track. There was no movement. No sign of life. She regretted not bringing her phone on her trip to get water. It was too still, too silent. The radiator rattled and Stella jumped, grabbing the girl's arm.

The teenager looked up for the first time since they entered the room. How long had they been sitting there? Her eyes were green and glistening. Stella hadn't heard her crying.

"Phone?" Stella mouthed, her lips forming an "O." The girl just stared. Stella mimicked texting. The girl shook her head, a tear breaking loose from the corner of her eye and falling to her chin. Somehow Stella had found the one teenager not glued to her cellphone.

Stella considered logging in to the computer. It sat there, dark and silent, an oracle awaiting her questions. A photograph was taped to the monitor. Two boys, their faces peeking out from beneath a pile of stuffed toys, arms wrapped tightly around each other. That's when she realized that she, too, was crying.

Stella sensed movement in the room and she turned. The girl held out a tissue, her hand reaching across the small space between them.

***

In the weeks following the attack, Stella would listen to politicians and pundits argue about the second amendment, about what is right, about what is *just*. She would hear their voices, loud with their certainty and conviction. And she would think back to that moment, in that empty room, with that trembling girl whose name she didn't know, and wonder if she could ever be certain of anything.

An Anthology

Cheryl Parisien

Cheryl Parisien is a Winnipeg Métis writer who studied creative writing with Dave Williamson and Uma Parameswaran. She's worked in magazine publishing for more than 20 years, writing many articles on varied topics. She currently works in communications. She's won awards for both her professional and creative writing and is affectionately known as "First Draft Cheryl" among her colleagues. "Veronica Hates Her Life" is from *Pineapples*, her first short story collection, currently seeking publication. Dave Williamson was her mentor during the writing of *Pineapples*. She is now working on a novel set during the Riel resistance.

Veronica Hates Her Life

Every morning, in the dark, Veronica got into her Volkswagen Rabbit and headed west, away from the sun, to a job in St. James that she hated. As she crossed the city, sometimes the moon was visible overhead, and she wished upon it as she passed under it, hoping for some kind of positive moon energy. Such wishful thinking was stupid, but that was what desperate people did.

There must be a way to endure this.

Too bad there wasn't a cliff to drive off but, on the prairies, the landscape didn't provide one.

She passed through Winnipeg's central hub at Portage Avenue and Main Street, onto the long artery of Portage Avenue that would carry her to her torment. The knot in her stomach formed and grew, the nearer she got to work. It wasn't healthy to live like this, but what was the alternative?

Her dissatisfaction began about a year earlier, with the built-up general malaise that most people felt about their jobs. She had been there for eleven years, which was feeling like at least three years too long. The work itself was not really the issue, although she was getting bored with it. Being a managing editor was great, and at one time it had been her dream job. But a few years in, the cracks of the place started to show. What bothered her most was the company culture, and her boss in particular.

Veronica had seen her share of abuse. Growing up, her mother yelled and called Veronica stupid all the time. Veronica could never do anything right, whether it was peeling potatoes "the wrong way" or how she wore her hair. Once, when she was fourteen, Veronica sat at the kitchen table painting her nails. No one else was home, and Veronica snacked on some peanuts while she worked. Veronica's mother came home and freaked out. She called Veronica stupid for eating peanuts and doing her nails at the same time. "The chemicals!" she'd screamed. She picked up the dish and emptied the peanuts in the trash. Veronica was too stunned to react; she grabbed her polish and ran to her room. She couldn't understand why her mother would react like that to something so harmless. A week later, Veronica came home from school and found her mother sitting at the kitchen table, painting her nails, and eating peanuts from the same dish. Veronica stared but said nothing.

Her first husband and dished out more of the same. He also called her stupid and criticized nearly everything she did. Veronica considered how children of alcoholics married alcoholics as adults. The idea seemed to have merit. Did she have a sign on her head or something? "Abuse me! Abuse me!" in blinking lights.

The workplace bullying started at her first publishing job, when she was working as a proofreader. Things were fine until new management came in and turned the workplace toxic. It started with quarterly reviews where the manager "didn't believe in" giving anyone a score higher than a three out of five in any category. When Veronica questioned this, she was singled out for extra "attention" by the manager and got in trouble all the time for no reason. She was moved away from her fellow proofreaders to a little-used annex; she was actually surprised her desk hadn't been moved to the maintenance closet. She stood it for a year and then took the underground railroad to a competing publisher. She detoxed there with fellow refugees of the same company and ended up being headhunted by a publisher in suburban St. James. The new job was everything she wanted, until it wasn't.

The signs were always there: nepotism, resistance to change, the inability of management to see things from another point of view. Her boss, a tall, grey-haired man who was pushing seventy and loved to complain about "political correctness," saw his small business as an extension of himself. Normal business transactions and events, like a client not renewing a contract or an employee quitting, were taken as personal slights. He was a hothead. He could go from calm to raging in milliseconds. Somehow, she had always skated by and avoided being the target of his attacks, but it was inevitable that her time would come. And so it did, one spring morning.

It was caused by an unreasonable client, one her boss often referred to as "a dick" he wanted to "punch out". She was fed up with having to surf this client's moods. She started grinding her teeth as she slept and cracked a tooth. She got a mouth guard but the tooth still hurt like hell when she chewed on that side. Anything crunchy was off the menu.

So the project in question was going through its umpteenth change, and her boss surprised her one morning, before she could sift through the pile of emails full of contradicting instructions from said client and asked about the progress. She was flustered and not perky enough about things, she supposed, when the volcano blew. Yelling, finger-pointing, eyes wild and flecks of spittle flying everywhere. She had to "adjust her attitude" (what?) and had to learn to "take it and like it" (double what?) when it came to the client's abuse. She was so frozen and scared that she could only gape. With his arms waving around, she thought her boss would have hit her if there hadn't been a desk between them. Panic took over. All she could think about was how he blocked her door so she couldn't escape. She was on the third floor, so there was no way she could break the glass and get out that way if she had to.

At one point he walked away, then spun around and came back for more yelling, because the first round wasn't enough. It was stunning, really. What was he so upset about? She hadn't complained about anything and hadn't refused to do the project. The rage came out of nowhere, and the surprise of it was what caused Veronica to freeze. The last editor who'd worked on the project complained incessantly and quit after a few months, but no one had ever told him to "adjust his attitude" or to take the abuse and like it. She sat alone in her office with her heart beating way too fast after the boss stalked off.

If ever there was a time to get in a car, drive away, and never look back, this was it. Too bad there was a mortgage to pay, and she was the main breadwinner of the house. Her new husband, Ron, was a self-employed IT consultant with an unreliable income. She was stuck with no way out, and no safety net. Why wasn't there a sabbatical she could take, to rest and recharge and feel like a person again? Was that too much to ask? She fantasized about getting cancer, for the respite.

In the weeks following *the incident*, she felt queasy all the time. Was she going to be fired? Were other people in the office talking about her? She was certain she heard people saying her name when they were talking in the hall. Her heart seized when she heard the whispering, and tried to parse what was being said. One time, she heard someone curse in exasperation when they spilled coffee. It wasn't anything dramatic, but the shock of it jolted her, and she had the shakes for the rest of the afternoon. She no longer had confidence in her abilities, and she couldn't judge what she should be worried about, or if she should even be worried at all. And that just led to more worry about the worry. Sleep was elusive. Fear gnawed her insides. She had to look up simple words because she didn't trust her spelling, even with spell-check. It was no way to live.

Her alarm clock on her bedside table was always five minutes fast. She had to adjust the time back every week, and every week it ended up the same. One morning she knocked over the water glass on her bedside table. The spilled water seeped under the alarm clock and with a zap and a spark, the glowing green numbers blinked out. She bought a new clock, a different brand this time, and the same five-minute time jump happened again. She wondered if her bedroom was in a bubble where time moved at a different rate. It would explain how her nights, even though full of fitful sleep, seemed to go by so fast. Ron was out working most nights installing a server for a new client, so she slept alone. She had a lot of time to woolgather. She thought about the nature of time a lot. She looked up Einstein's works on relativistic time and even thought she understood it.

It was still too cold and icy out for her to go on her usual lunchtime walks through neighbouring Assiniboine Park. The fresh air and exercise usually cleared her head, but the trails she liked were full of ankle-deep puddles of muddy water and slushy ice. Staying inside the office was suffocating. Aside from the busted heating and mice dropping from the ceiling tiles, the oppressive atmosphere was too much. Instead, she got in her car and escaped to nearby Polo Park Mall, parked in the covered lot, and listened to the radio while she ate lunch in her cold car, and phoned everyone she could think of for job leads. As she spoke with each person, with forced cheerfulness, clinging to hope that, this time, something would bear fruit, her breath formed little clouds of icy fog that hung inside the car. Each call was a dead end, and she was left sitting in a nebula of defeat.

She applied for other jobs. She had valuable skills, right? She went on a few interviews, but nothing panned out. Either she never made the cut, or the pay was abysmal. So it was show up, keep your head down, and try not to have a heart attack when you heard him stomping down the hall. She was attuned to everyone's footsteps. She was going to get an ulcer. Would getting into a car accident be so bad? There were worse things. It was one way to be off work for a while. She no longer exercised or cared what she ate – when she had an appetite, that is.

One night she woke up at three in the morning with pain across her midsection. It was as if a rubber band was tightening across her stomach and back, squeezing her in two. No matter which way she moved, onto her right side or her left, she could find no relief. She got up, took some antacid and walked laps around her apartment. Walking took her mind off the pain and seemed to ease it a bit. The next day, she went to her doctor. After an ultrasound, she learned she had to get her gallbladder out, and right away.

She was admitted to hospital later that week and wasn't really worried about the surgery. The threat of ill health was a comfort compared to the uncertainty she'd been living with. Surgery was simple, with a beginning and an end. As she was wheeled into the operating room, under the bright lights and masked faces, she choked back a laugh. The sound was hollow and out of place in the sterile white room. The anesthesiologist gave her a curious look. He was covered in a blue gown, mask, and cap, and all she could make out were his bushy brown eyebrows sitting above his grey eyes like fat caterpillars. He asked what was so funny. He hadn't even administered any drugs yet. The caterpillars wriggled. She was laughing because all she could think about was how her boss had said her surgery was inconvenient since this was their busy time, and how it would be better for him if she could have her surgery over the weekend instead. She'd said it didn't work like that, she had no say, and anyway it was a bit of a serious situation. But she didn't tell that to the anesthesiologist.

"I guess I'm just nervous," she said.

The caterpillars relaxed and his gloved hand raised a mask of hissing gas over her nose and mouth. He told her to count backwards from one hundred. She didn't break eye contact with him as she counted, and when she got to ninety-seven the caterpillars turned into teal butterflies and flew away, up and out of the operating room. Then everything went black.

The best part about the surgery was the recovery. She was off work for two weeks and ate Jello a lot. Her husband took care of her, helping her to get out of bed and walk around the apartment. She did laps, leaning on Ron for support. It was kind of a nice time.

When she went back to her job, all the backed-up work was waiting for her. No card, no flowers, no one asking how she was. It was straight to business. There were deadlines. By the end of that first day, it was as if she'd never left. She wondered what other internal organs she could get rid of. What did the spleen do, anyway? How many more days off could she get if it were removed? She saw herself as a collection of disposable parts. Not everything was necessary, if you really thought about it. There were redundancies. She pressed her hands to her side, over her healing, itchy scars. She imagined ripping open the stitches and rooting around inside for something to pull out and discard. Everything felt extraneous.

She stared out her office window. The snow was nearly all melted now, the trees bare, the new leaves still hidden. Hazy clouds hung in the sky, not seeming to move. It felt like everything was in stasis. Full spring would never come. The world would stay lifeless.

Each day she went to work, she smiled, nodded, and pretended to be alive.

She returned to her parking spot in the mall lot for lunch. She didn't need to run the motor much anymore to keep it warm inside. She was used to the cold, anyway.

"If you bear it long enough, you can become accustomed to almost anything," she said to her empty car.

There was no anger in her voice, only weariness, and that was more frightening than anything.

Maddie Lock

German-born Maddie Lock fell in love with words as she learned the English language. Maddie graduated with a BA in English Lit before sidetracking into the business world. In 2014, Maddie returned to her first love and published two children's books, one a Royal Palm Award winner. Her essays have appeared in *Gravel*, *Wanderlust-Journal* and 2020 Anthology, *The RavensPerch*, *Under the Sun*, *Ruminate*, *Brevity*, and the Unleash Press *Conversations* anthology among others. She recently completed a historical memoir about her German roots. Find out more at www.maddielock.com.

WORC

When I was fifteen, I walked up to the Whataburger on Seminole Boulevard at the edge of our lower middle class neighborhood in Seminole, Florida and applied for a carhop position. My family had moved into a rental house a few months earlier and I needed a job. My stepfather Ted had recently retired after twenty years in the army. His highly specialized technical and tactical skills as a Chief Warrant Officer did not transition well into the civilian job market, and after a long and fruitless search he had taken a job on the assembly line at Open Road Campers. His wage was $1.60 an hour, the minimum in 1971. My German mother, Susi, had no marketable skills except housekeeping and also had two young children at home besides me. She had attended school until the age of fourteen, then stayed home to take care of her siblings. Ted's army pension was barely enough for a family of five. If I wanted clothes, toiletries, makeup, and mad money I needed to earn it myself.

Up until this time, I lived a life of leisure. My mother had grown up in a broken family during and after WWII. As the oldest, she had been responsible for her five siblings while her mother worked as a seamstress and a housekeeper. Her four sisters and one brother called her "little mother." As parents tend to do, she wanted to give me a different life, and the only chore I had was to walk our long-haired dachshund Bitsy. When I wasn't in school, I mostly lay around on my bed, writing stories and reading books by the score. The library became my second home. On weekends, I woke up, peed, fluffed my pillow, and settled in with a current read.

Sometimes Mom brought me French toast and a glass of milk. When I finally headed to the library for new reading material, she would pluck my clothes from the floor, and make my bed. The downside to all this care was that I felt like a stranger everywhere else in the house. When I stepped into the kitchen for a snack or a drink, my mother flew in behind me, demanding to know what I was doing. Mom kept her home spotless, and lounging around in the living room was not an option for me.

I don't remember how long I worked at Whataburger, but I do know I passed a summer vacation working nearly every day. I met the kids in my neighborhood. One of the boys had built a wooden go-cart, and he would wend his way through the neighborhood streets and pull in with a flair. At the end of my shift I often climbed into the boxy thing with him for a ride home. But not straight home. At the other end of the neighborhood were empty fields, a place for the local teens to hang out, drink Boones Farm Strawberry Hill, and toke the occasional reefer. My ego flush with tips, I exuded a new kind of confidence, a security that comes with accomplishment, of feeling purposeful. I was helping myself and my family. When I looked into the mirror I had a new glow, even with bad hair and looks that didn't quite fit in as I worked on assimilating into the 70's culture so different from the army base in Fukuoka, Japan, where I had lived just a few months before.

***

Etymologically, the early word *work* as a verb is closely associated with *labor*, and was advocated (by those who needed laborers) as *a way to alleviate poverty*. Many definitions seem to align with negative connotations: *weorc* or *worc* has an Indo-European stem of *werg* *(to do)* via Greek *ergon:* action without punitive connotations, and the Latin *urgere:* to press or bear down, or compel. Add in *wrikan:* to persecute, and *wrecan* as in wreak havoc. The German word *Arbeit* connotes hardship and suffering.

As a noun, the Old English *worc*, c.1200, is defined as "something done, a discrete act, action, *products of labor, toil, physical effort or exertion.* Also from c.1200 comes *artistic labor—*

better, but could this be a reference to the labor applied to the physical creation of architecture and churches which was nothing more than toil as "extreme or exhausting work"?

Or as a reference to the painters, such as Giotto, who labored in creating the beautiful frescoes inside them? *Scholarly labor* shows up c.1200 as well, perhaps later in reference to the scribes who painstakingly copied existing *artistic works. Work of art* shows up in 1774 and refers to artistic *creation.* Interestingly, *to be out of work* is from the 1590s. Wonder what they called it earlier? *Work ethic* shows up as late as 1959. Look up synonyms for work and you find a whole new list: *slog, drudgery, sweat, exertion, travail, servitude, grindstone, donkey work.* Yikes.

From that Whataburger job onward I worked. Many meanings of the word touched me in some way. I *created* ice cream sundaes at Dairy Queen; exerted *physical effort* as a stockperson at McCrory's; I demonstrated my *work ethic* as a desk clerk *drudge* (so boring) at Allstate for part of the day and *sweated* while flipping burgers at McDonald's at night, then moved on to *servitude* waiting tables at Gi-Gi's Italian Restaurant as I attended English and creative writing courses in college (*scholarly labor*) and realized my writing could be an *artistic creation.* The Thesaurus lists a couple positive synonyms: *endeavor, performance, drive,* which are the words I took to heart.

***

After graduating from USF with a degree in English Lit, the challenge became how to make a living, because I didn't want to toil for someone else anymore. I wanted to support myself with my creative work. A few local magazines gave me freelance assignments. I loved the research, interviews, and working on deadlines to create an article. Always goal driven, I especially loved the byline and felt a sense of accomplishment. But the money wasn't there. I moved to Orlando for better job opportunities, and answered an ad from the Winter Park Observer, a community paper, for a classified ad salesperson. The plan was to impress the editor with my writing skills and have him beg me to join their reporting staff. In the meantime, I would have a steady income. Although I didn't have any sales skills I was hired. And my life turned. I reveled in helping customers market their businesses and sold a lot of ads. This led to other sales jobs, each time a move up and forward; from outside ad sales to office building solutions. Until I eventually ended up *out of work.*

And felt I had lost an important part of me.

Here's what happened. I had taken a job with Comcast Sound Communications, where I met my future husband. After three years we married, and I soon became pregnant. My high-stress position as an account executive demanded a 50+ hour work week, along with evening network functions, and sales conferences. After my son was born, I took one blissful month off and then hurried back part-time to take care of my clients. After a few months I was back to a full schedule. This was a career I loved. In the 1990's Comcast had a thriving division that provided commercial sound environments, such as background music, noise masking, or white noise, and paging. I had built a good account base and made rounds within my territory daily. At this time, it was still possible, and essential, for face to face visits. Customers became friends; we did lunches and swapped Orlando Magic tickets. I made my own schedule, had freedom throughout the day, and felt like my own boss. I also made decent money. Actually, good money. A win-win situation I found deeply satisfying and enjoyable.

Until one day it wasn't.

I had hired a kind and experienced nanny a few months after Jay was born. She fell in love with my cheerful son and I felt secure with her care of him. When I wasn't at work, I hung out with Jay. I hurried home in the afternoons, and switched gears from numbers and meetings to saturating myself with toddler smiles and wet kisses. Jay opened up a magical world for me and taught me to see things from a child's innocent and wondrous perspective. I remember one night we walked into the front yard to gaze up at the full moon, when suddenly my son exclaimed AAAAH! and jumped a few feet away. He focused on something in front of him, but I couldn't see anything. Then I realized he was fascinated with his shadow. When he moved, it moved with him. To see the realization come over him that this was somehow a part of him, was priceless.

But it wasn't, couldn't, be enough, these special times. When I found myself too frazzled at the end of the day to give my best to those who mattered most, I knew I had to make a change. My husband had become a necessary but often neglected shadow. So I gave notice at my beloved corporate job. I resolved to stay home and become a proper mother. Find time to be a wife again. A different kind of work; a different identity. A *work in progress*, for now.

So Jay and I spent our days together. We sat at the kitchen table with bright crayons and attempted to color pictures within the lines. We hung out in the pool, Jay in his floating duck and me floating on my back beside him, making faces while he laughed uncontrollably. We threw a ball in the yard, both of us trying to throw straight. I pushed him in a tree swing which made him giggle and scream. We made daily trips around our neighborhood in his stroller and met every person and every dog. We sat on our back deck, Jay in his high chair picking at bits of fruit and sharing them with me. We watched Barney the Purple dinosaur in the afternoons; Jay learned to mimic Barney's opening theme and was entranced as he rocked back and forth attempting to sing the Barney song. We looked at lots of books. I read and pointed to the words while he stared and pointed along, his mouth trying to form what he heard. We even braved Chuck E. Cheese, once. I put together play dates, during which I did my best to learn insights from the other moms.

For a while my son and I did great together. But after a few months, we both became restless. Or perhaps I did, and he felt it. We started getting cranky with each other which left me feeling like a bad mother. Jay was delighted when his father came home in the evenings; I even thought he looked relieved. Here was a new face, new fun to be had. Or maybe I told myself that to get over the guilt of my restlessness.

I needed more. And that sucked. Why couldn't I be content being a mother all day and a wife at night? Instead, I felt I had lost a part of myself; that I was *working against* an inherent need, a part of my identity. Enervated, and feeling as if my inner self was a bit dimmer, fading perhaps, I knew I had to make a change. This staying home stuff was not working for me. I would do myself –and my son—a great disservice if we continued like we were. But I also didn't want to go back to my high-stress job. So I expanded my love of old things and opened an antique store in a tony section of town. I opened at 11:00 and closed at 4:00, catering to well-off housewives and interior decorators who would do their business during these hours.

For childcare I recruited GaGa (my son's name for his paternal grandmother) who was delighted with her free reign to spoil her newest grandchild. Coming home one afternoon, I pulled up in front of our house and there was my son still in pajamas, hair sticking out in every direction and wearing new cowboy boots. He had a broom under him and was galloping around the front yard. His mouth was ringed with a rainbow of colors, something sugary, which I did not allow. Clearly he was having a blast. Perhaps this was what he needed all along?

Soon I felt it was time for pre-school, at least a couple days a week. I found a local church daycare with intimate classes and signed up. The first day I took him there is seared in my memory wherever guilt is stored. I carried my happy and secure son to his new classroom. We stood and gawked at the kids and toys and general mayhem which looked like so much fun. He was delighted. Until I started to hand him over to his teacher. Jay's body went rigid, his eyes swiveled to me in a panic and I felt a warmth through his diapers; he had released his bladder in fear. The director rushed me out, saying that it was best to make a clean break. Assurances from the director were firm and confident: *all children go through this, the teachers know how to distract them quickly. He'll be fine.* I left. And promptly threw up in the bushes by the front door.

When I pulled up to the church that afternoon, I saw him at the window, his hand on the crank, opening and closing the jalousies, clearly fascinated with the mechanics. Our eyes met and he broke into a grin. The next time I dropped him off he hesitated only briefly, then ran to a new friend. *Hmm, I thought, he sure adapted fast.* My ego was bruised, although I felt relief that I wouldn't be spewing my breakfast into the bushes again. But I had my doubts about his supervision. So I recruited a wonderful elderly woman who lived down the street from us and had raised a bunch of her own kids. Ms. Ellie stayed with us until we moved and Jay began Kindergarten. She taught him new words, big words, and insisted on perfect annunciation. She taught him how to hold and eat with a fork in a neat and elegant manner. She pointed to the planes that flew overhead to land at the nearby Orlando airport and made up stories of where they may be coming from. This was her purpose, as in *working up* or to "bring by labor or special effort to a higher state or condition." (from the 1660s).

In turn, I was able to regain the part of me that needed to be vital outside of the home, a purpose that belonged to me alone. In my little antique business I created displays, kept the shop immaculate, played Benny Goodman through overhead speakers, and attended estate auctions. I chatted up my customers and always had a story to tell them about any certain piece. Although I closed the shop after two years and went back to work in sales for a while, I missed being my own boss and eventually started another business, a security systems integration company that turned into a lucrative family business. Throughout the years, beginning with that Whataburger job, I deeply felt the power of work as *purpose*. Being a mother and wife gave me shared purpose, but I needed more. Having my own business provided the perfect amount of individual identity. Ms. Ellie had infinite patience, loved teaching my son, and was able to fulfill her purpose. And she allowed me to fulfill mine.

***

Our passion drives our purpose; feeling strong emotions for something motivates us. Sometimes we know from an early age what our passion is and find a way to pursue it with purpose. For others it changes throughout the years. I've been multiple women with multiple passions. Sometimes they overlapped. My passion for providing quality products and services gave me purpose, so much that I was compelled to start my own small business providing security and life safety systems. I provided employment, embraced fair and ethical practices, and offered a comfortable work environment with good pay. It supported me and my family. My purpose began with that Whataburger carhop job; with the power of self-sufficiency. My passions shifted throughout the years, but the purpose remained constant.

Eventually, the desire to write returned; I rediscovered my passion for *artistic creation*, and I wrote and published two children's books about dogs, another passion with an important purpose. When I discovered a long-held family secret and was asked to write about it, passion and purpose turned me towards memoir and creative non-fiction. Reading excellent literary journals created a desire to become an essayist. I took classes and began working on my ten thousand hours toward excellence. After twenty years of fostering our company, the difficult decision was made to sell it. My husband and I each had artistic passions to devote our time to: he with music and me with my writing.

Writing is *hard work*, more difficult than anything I have done before, not only in learning and applying the skills needed for excellence— the hours upon hours of classes and practice— but something more. I've spent way too much time ruminating over this fact. After years of confidently selling products and services within the framework of a company (either mine or someone else's) do I question everything I write and submit? Is it good enough? How can it be better?

I well remember the ka-thunk of my heart as my shaky finger hovered over the SUBMIT button for my first essay. How I hesitated over and over and wondered why anyone would want to read what I wrote. (I still get nervous when I submit, just less so.) And why now, while always trying to write the truest possible words, do I question the honesty of what I write? I've concluded that, because I write creative nonfiction, my feelings emanate from the deeply personal aspect of putting myself and my life "out there." The product now is me, which can make rejection feel personal. In the writing world, we are taught to differentiate between the author and the story's narrator, but the reader may not be aware of this. When, after reading my latest essay my friends say wow, I had no idea! and look at me as if they have been let in on a closely held secret, I cringe inside, just a bit. But not enough to stop. Purpose drives my passion. I well remember the brief euphoria and lasting sense of satisfaction when I published the first book, and when I received my first essay acceptance.

Worc belongs to a part of our self-identity. Doing anything to the best of our abilities gives us the sense of accomplishment, and purpose that we all need. Even a carhop job.

An Anthology

Edward M. Cohen

Edward M. Cohen's story collection, *Before Stonewall*, was published by Awst Press; his novel, *$250,000* by G.P. Putnam's Sons; his novella, *A Visit to my Father with my Son*, by Running Wild Press; and his chapbook, *Grim Gay Tales*, by Fjords Review.

Fishman Paper Box Co., Inc.

Originally published in the September 1965 issue of Evergreen Review

Fishman heaved his hulking body over the side of his bed and stumbled through the dark, silent apartment, losing his way, banging into walls, searching for the light switch, washing, dressing, combing his hair without looking.

Numbly, he performed his morning chores; tied his tie, gathered his wallet, keys, and handkerchief, wrapped his throat in a muffler, his body in an overcoat, his plump hands into gloves. He turned off the light and lumbered down the stairs and into his car.

For twenty-six years, since 1930, he had traveled, in the same lonely manner, to and from the same Brooklyn loft and his unchanging Brooklyn apartment. He moved through his narrow world; apartment, car, office … as if it were a long, depressing railroad flat and the short drive every day was like plodding down the hallway from one dark room to another.

Vaguely he remembered the early days, when he had first opened the plant, how the square sign on the door, "Fishman Paper Box Co., Inc.," had thrilled him, how the obsequiousness of the elevator operator had defined his new status every morning, how he had nursed each new machine into being with clumsy, loving hands.

He parked his car directly in front of the entrance, entered the elevator and nodded sleepily to the operator. It was a cavernous, rattling freight elevator, gated on two open sides with crisscrossing metal. The overbearing depth and height of it, equipped to handle the freight of all the tenants in the large factory building, intimidated Fishman and he did not like the way conversations echoed aimlessly through the space.

On Work

"Kinda cold for November," the aged operator said. He had not changed in the twenty-six years either, but the early respect for Fishman had been replaced with deadened familiarity.

"November," Fishman sighed unhappily, shivering in the cold of the open-air chute, "November." Christmas was coming. Oy.

The elevator lurched to a stop. The metal gate jangled open. Fishman walked through the outer office, nodded to his secretary, Beatrice, and entered his own dingy prison with a moan.

"Oy, November."

November, at Fishman's place, was an unending nightmare of screaming customers, impossible schedules and constant crises. Each year, as orders grew larger, deadlines tighter, tempers shorter, Fishman and his machinery crept closer and closer to obsolescence.

Going into the office every morning was like stepping into a swamp. Miserably, he glanced at the mud green walls, and the slimy Venetian blinds. Clots of yellowed papers crammed the bookshelves. Moldy samples buried the heavy, black leather couch in the corner.

He sank into his chair, behind a desk heaped with the stale residue of yesterday's crises; bills not yet paid, orders not yet shipped, supplies not yet arrived. He searched through the junk for his breakfast, unwrapped his roll, and uncapped his coffee.

"Beatrice!" he shouted, rearing his head back and cracking the bones in his neck. "Can't you clear up my desk in the morning? How can a man think like this?"

"Yeah," she sneered from the outer office, not interrupting the clatter of her aged typewriter, "And with my extra hand, I'll sweep the floor."

Savagely chewing on his roll, he cursed her under his breath. The jangling phone jarred him and he stared at the flickering light button, measuring the time it took her to answer.

"Hello, Fishman's," she droned. "Just a minute, Mr. Kleinfeld, I'll see if he's in."

Fishman's body coiled for attack. He stared belligerently at the intercom, daring it to buzz. Of course, it did not.

"Kleinfeld on 600," Beatrice screamed from the outer office. "Are you in?"

Fishman slapped his hand against his brow, popped out of his chair and stomped to the doorway, shouting.

"How many times do I have to tell you, use the intercom? We have to scream at each other like this is the Fulton Fish Market?"

"Oh God," Beatrice whined, "I can see what kind of a day this is going to be."

"What the hell did I have it installed for?"

"Look Fishman," she answered, "do me a favor. Get me no fancy gadgets, you hear? I've got enough on my mind, the way it is."

"You know what that cost me?"

"It only means extra work. That's all."

"What kind extra work?" he sputtered in amazement, fury flushing his face.

Suddenly, she spun in her chair and screamed at him with equal passion. "Push the hold button! Push this button! Push that button! Will you leave me alone before I go crazy?"

"Jesus Christ!"

"Listen," she said sharply, "do you want to talk to Kleinfeld or not? Just answer that."

He sneered at her, baring his teeth in a hateful grin, "And if I didn't want to talk to Kleinfeld?" he asked. "How would I not, since he's heard every word you said?"

"He hasn't heard a thing," she answered, pointing to the receiver, pressed between her breasts.

Fishman snorted and paced back to his desk. He snapped the receiver from the phone and snarled into it.

"Look Fishman," Kleinfeld fumed, "where the hell are my Seduction boxes?"

"What Seduction boxes?"

"Don't play games with me!" screeched Kleinfeld. Fishman held the phone from his ear. "Did we talk yesterday? Did you tell me Seduction was on the truck? Did you?"

"Sure."

"So where the hell are they if they were on the truck? Missouri?"

"You didn't get them?"

"Did I ever get a box when promised? Did you, once in your life, ever keep your word?"

"Kleinfeld, cut it out. The Seduction boxes are there."

"You miserable sonofabitch. They are not!"

"Listen, Kleinfeld, those boxes were on the truck yesterday and they were delivered yesterday and if you want a signed receipt, I'll shove it down your throat!"

"What am I, crazy?"

"Kleinfeld, you've got the crummiest receiving department in the world. Those idiots don't know a delivery's been made for months."

"Fishman, I'm sitting with a seven-hundred-dollar perfume order that can't be shipped without Seduction."

"Kleinfeld, check on your morons!"

"Fishman, if they're not here, I'll never give you another stick of business, believe me."

"Don't you threaten me at nine o'clock in the morning!" Fishman yelled. "Did I take my coat off yet? Did I open the mail? Did I drink my coffee? I have to listen to your crap before I even breathe? I'll drop dead on you! In spite of Christmas!"

He flung the receiver back on the phone.

"Beatrice!"

"Yeah?"

"What's with Kleinfeld's Seduction?"

"It's scheduled for the machine this morning," she answered.

"Jesus Christ," he moaned, dropping his head into his hands.

The hours slipped by this way, with unnerving rapidity, as had every hour for the last twenty-six years. Fishman bellowed from one end of the plant to the other, cursing the machinery, threatening to die, insulting the employees. Three girls from the production line were out sick. The blade on the cutting machine broke down and he spent half an hour writhing in anguish while his idiot machinist tried to fix it. A new girl made two hundred boxes with the label upside down. The foreman had forgotten to order glue and they had barely enough for the day.

The phone rang constantly and Beatrice hollered for him all over the plant, never once using the intercom. His creditors wanted payment. His customers wanted shipments. His competitors were undercutting him. His suppliers couldn't deliver. He screamed into the phone and then held the receiver away from his ear when the screaming boomeranged.

He told the Maskulyne Pipe people that the boxes were on the truck, but he took them off to deliver Seduction so that, by the time Kleinfeld was sure the boxes weren't there, they would be on the way to him.

The stuttering, archaic machines spewed forth boxes regularly and rapidly onto the dark, rotting floor, into the hands of bored, glassy-eyed workers.

At one o'clock, Beatrice screamed for him across the entire loft.

"Fishman! Lunch!"

He walked past the long table of girls toward his office. Henry, the machinist, skipped along behind him, wiping his glasses constantly, a nervous smile twitching at the corners of his mouth. Fishman's body was contorted in disgust. Tense creases pulled at his mouth and spattered his face in curlicues. His eyes peered spitefully over the shoulders of the girls, hungering for an error on which to pounce, checking the delicate movement of their hands. Henry talked frantically in a squealing voice laced with giggles and Fishman answered him thickly, biting into each word and spraying forth saliva. He walked faster and faster toward Beatrice, shooing Henry off with his hand.

"The cutter is finished! Done! Over! Fishman! You hear me? Finished! Done! Kaput!"

"Fix it! What the hell am I paying you for?"

"It needs a complete overhaul, Fishman! Complete! Overhaul! Fishman!"

"I haven't got time for an overhaul. Fix whatever is wrong and don't bother me!"

Henry giggled shrilly and fluttered his horrified hands to his face.

"It's falling apart!" he shrieked.

They had reached the door to the office where Beatrice waited, arms crossed over her bosom.

"Henry!" he bellowed, "Don't bother me! I need that machine and I need it this afternoon or I'm out of business! I don't care if it's tied together with ribbon!"

He wheeled past Beatrice into his office and left the machinist laughing frantically at the door.

He paced back and forth, mopping his perspiring brow while Beatrice set out two paper napkins, one for him and one for her, and on them placed their thick pastrami sandwiches, wrapped in greasy, waxed paper. They both had soggy containers of coffee and, in the center, she made a symmetrical design of pickles, mustard dripping out of slimy green paper cones, coleslaw in tiny, ridged cups, packets of sugar for his coffee, and thin wooden sticks to mix with.

Covered by white cardboard triangles, set off to the side, were two slabs of chocolate cream pie, whipped cream oozing out of the sides.

"All right, Fishman. Sit."

They ate silently, sitting across the desk from each other. They unfolded their sandwiches, squeezed out the mustard, each took a pickle, sipped on their coffee. He loaded his with sugar and mixed it mechanically. She drank hers nearly white with milk. He squeezed his coleslaw on top of the pastrami as part of the sandwich. She nibbled from the paper cup. They chomped away without a word, staring into the depths of pastrami while chewing, as if selecting the best angle for the next attack.

After finishing one half of the sandwich, Beatrice paused, wiped her lips and sipped on the coffee but Fishman grabbed directly for the second upon completion of the first and, after the second, reached for another, surprised that he had finished both halves.

He thought about box making, the orders in work while eating. He planned to run a Christmas candy box that afternoon, a difficult job with a die-cut top, and he pictured the board being cut, deposited on the machine, moving swiftly on a conveyor belt under brushes dripping with gray glue, traveling past girls who covered it with a colorful wrap, down to the stamper which formed the box in one heavy pound.

The tops and bottoms were made on different machines and the girls put them together along a wooden table, passing them from one to the other; glue, inside the spine, edges trimmed, glue, outside spine, edges trimmed. The last girl wiped them clean of excess glue like Fishman removed the whipped cream from his lips with a napkin and the box was as finished as the lunch, only the pastrami-stained paper, the whipped cream-tinged triangle, the soggy containers, and one pickle left for Beatrice to clear before going on to the next aggravation of the day.

He lit a cigar while she cleaned up, ignoring the flicker of distaste that passed over her face. Such an ugly face, he thought, had to have something to complain about.

He had hired her fifteen years ago because of her ugliness. Pretty women, he felt, had no place in an office. He mistrusted them. They never worked. They caused trouble among the laborers and, if it ever happened that one turned out smart, she was too smart to stay.

Beatrice's face was pockmarked and jowly; her eyebrows thick, her nose flat, her lips wide, her teeth yellow. Her hair was an ugly dirty blonde, kinky and unmanageable. Her chin sagged into breasts, into the stomach, into thighs and she never bothered to shave her hairy legs.

She left the room with the garbage. He belched and leaned back in his chair, blowing smoke rings, continuing to reflect on Beatrice. When he didn't have to look at her, it was easier to see her redeeming qualities.

She fought like a demon for the company, intimidated creditors calling for money, scanned the bills with her squinting, tiny eyes for overcharges, and never let one get by. Lazy, lying, disrespectful, to be sure, he concluded, but one way or the other, she got the work done.

"Hey Beatrice!" he called. "We've got a million things to do. Can you work late?"

"Oy Fishman," she moaned, "I've got a sick mother."

"And the billing we haven't done?" he sneered. "And the letters? And the checks to do? They're not important?"

"Fishman, I'm tired today."

"Tired!" he roared, pounding his hand on the desk. "You think I'm not tired? Why don't we close the place and all go home to sleep?"

"All right, Fishman, all right."

"Doesn't anybody give a damn but me?" he mumbled.

"I said all right!" she screeched.

The phone rang. The afternoon started.

It was Shulman, the glue man. Fishman listened to Beatrice talking to him, explaining the emergency, ordering the glue, and pleading that it be delivered that afternoon. Then there was silence. Beatrice was listening and Fishman squirmed in his seat.

He heard Beatrice sputter apologetically into the phone. He could feel the perspiration twirling around the hair of his armpits as her efforts got more and more desperate and, apparently, Shulman remained adamant. Huge clots of pastrami floated around his insides in a sea of gastric juices and the taste of the chocolate pie shot up into his nose.

"Fishman!" she called, "Shulman wants C.O.D."

He lunged for the phone and caught Shulman in the middle of a familiar harangue. "Five thousand dollars is five thousand dollars, Beatrice darling. Am I a bank? Am I General Motors? Fishman, are you on?"

"Yeah-"

"Do you hear?"

"Do I hear? Do I hear? What else do I ever hear from you but complaints?"

"Fishman, you owe me five thousand dollars. Am I a bank?"

"Am I General Motors?" Fishman mocked.

"I have help to pay too, Fishman. I've got my own bills. I'm a small man, Fishman. Can I afford to carry you for so much?"

"Will you stop crying? Ship the goddam glue and I'll give you a check next week."

"Aw, Fishman, is that fair of you to ask? Beatrice, is that fair he should ask?"

"Beatrice, get off the phone," Fishman snarled. "She's got plenty to do, Shulman, without listening to your garbage."

"To you, its garbage, to me, its blood," Shulman answered in the endless whine. "When you give me a check, I'll ship the glue."

"You want to put me out of business?" Fishman hissed.

"Aw, Fishman -"

"If I don't have the glue, I don't have a plant and you'll eat your five thousand dollars!"

His body was huddled over the desk, his hands were so clammy the receiver kept slipping. Saliva dripped from his chin into the ashtray, turning the remnants of his cigar into mush. "You got another customer all of a sudden who pays better?"

"Fishman, I love you—"

On Work

"Don't love me, you bastard, ship! For twenty-six years, since 1930, I'm buying from you.
AND paying your ridiculous prices. AND letting you gyp me on weights. AND putting up
with your sloppy service. You've got the nerve to tell me C.O.D.?"

"Fishman, am I a bank?"

"Am I General Motors?" Fishman howled, slamming the receiver down in the middle of
Shulman's answer. For a moment, he sat panting over the phone, fists clenched on the desk,
head throbbing with pain, breath escaping from his mouth in sobs.

"Gimme an aspirin!" he called.

Kleinfeld's boxes were delivered and Maskulyne was loaded for the following day. The glue
arrived on the clanging elevator and the Christmas candy boxes started running.

For the last hour of the day, Fishman disappeared from sight. The doctor had advised him to
take a daily nap, but he had found a practice more relaxing.

He retreated to a special corner in the back of the plant. Hidden by shelves, he perched on a
carton, undid his shoelaces, and massaged his aching ankles. He pressed his nose to the
surrounding cardboard and peered spitefully through a crack, straining his vision until his
eyeballs ached, scribbling notes on the back of an envelope.

Two girls at the table talked constantly and he made a note to separate them. One girl went to
the bathroom three times and he made a note to fire her. Bulbs had blown over the workbench
and he made a note to fix them.

He kept his eyes on a new girl, a short, skinny creature with hair set in a cap of bobby-pinned
curls, thin-penciled eyebrows, and lipstick stretching over her lips so that her mouth met her
nose in a perpetual sneer.

She was the first at the table and one of her chores was to hop off the stool and gather boxes from the base of the machine. She did this with a flurry of motion and, when she went low for the boxes, her tight pants curled around her buttocks in revealing creases.

She was not to be trusted, Fishman thought, watching her intensely, waiting for one false move, hoping to catch her stealing, absently rubbing at his crotch.

Even when his inventory figures revealed no shortages, Fishman was plagued with visions of employees sneaking out full cartons of raw materials to sell cheaply to his competitors and even Beatrice and Henry, the oldest and most faithful, were not free from the shadow of his suspicion.

Vaguely, he felt robbed. He switched his glance to the worn, threading rubber on the conveyor belts, the awkward, old-fashioned, patched-together sections of metal which sparkled in the light.

Far across the plant, Henry puttered with the broken cutter and Fishman was forced to agree with the machinist's initial opinion. He squirmed in his mildewed corner, tense and unhappy, and turned his eyes from the sight. The cutter was finished, over, kaput. Even a complete overhaul, Fishman sighed wearily, could not bring it back to life.

He was startled by the five o'clock buzzer and immediately checked his watch to make sure some sneak hadn't pushed the signal ahead. He slipped out of his hiding place to be on the floor while the crew left, glancing into handbags and watching for bulging pockets, infuriated at the way the buzzer brought the deadened girls to life.

All day long, they walked around with sour expressions, tired, bored, complaining in dulled voices about headaches, sick mothers, overwork. But five o'clock comes, he simmered, and they giggle and shout, grab for their coats, full of life, suddenly happy and oh, feeling so much better. He stood by the time clock, rigid with fury, sneering as they filled the elevator with chatter and laughter.

He waited until the sounds were completely gone, swallowed by the elevator chute and vomited onto the street. Beatrice kept working and the racket of her typewriter resounded through the silence. Henry skipped around the floor, turning off lights, putting away tools, making an elaborate display of his efficiency and Fishman wandered about after him, straightening whatever Henry had touched.

The machinist yoo-hooed goodbye to Beatrice before taking the elevator down and his voice echoed through the gloomy deadness. Fishman stood alone in the dark, suddenly out of breath, lulled by Beatrice's steady clatter into sleepiness, straining his eyes to scan the machines, checking the parts, glancing unhappily at the broken cutter, trying to anticipate what would break down next.

He ran his hand soothingly over metal, too tired to conceal the affection he felt. The machines looked like corpses in the dark; three ghostly outlines of aged women, so drained of life that their skeletons projected eerily through their skin.

"Rest," he mumbled, "rest."

His eyelids fell heavily over his eyes. His body sagged in exhaustion. Pulsating pains flickered in his head.

He walked slowly to the office and stood for a moment in the doorway, staring silently at Beatrice, until she sensed his presence and turned around in shock.

"Oy, you scared me," she giggled. "This place gives me the creeps at night. God knows, some drunk could come up the backstairs anytime and, if I screamed, would anyone hear me?"

"Beatrice," he moaned.

"You could hear a pin drop, it gets so quiet and it's so dark in the back, I get palpitations."

"Beatrice, I've got a terrible headache. Clear off the couch, will you?"

"Oy, Fishman."

"Beatrice!"

"All right," she sighed, standing up, rubbing her back and wrinkling her face into an ugly expression of pain.

Fishman lingered at the door, giving her time to get ready, breathing hoarsely and dribbling onto his chin. When he heard her rustling noises cease, he slipped off his pants and joined her on the couch.

"All right, Fishman," she said in farewell, standing up abruptly, smoothing out her skirt, and heading back to her own desk in the outer office.

He sat on the couch, staring blankly ahead, anxious for her to go. He could hear her straightening out her desk, rummaging through her pocketbook, reaching for her coat. He lowered his face into his hands and massaged his temples, surprised that his headache still lingered.

She punched out and took the stairs down, it was too late for elevator service, and he heard the heavy metal door clang shut in a way that told him it hadn't locked.

"That's right," he sneered, forcing the words through the numbness creeping over his tongue. "Leave it open so they can rob me blind overnight."

Sue Mell

Sue Mell is a writer from Queens, NY. She earned her MFA from Warren Wilson, and was a 2020 BookEnds fellow at SUNY Stony Brook. Her debut novel, *Provenance,* won Madville Publishing's 2021 Blue Moon Novel Award and was chosen as a 2022 Great Group Read by the Women's National Book Association. Her collection of micro essays, *Giving Care*, won the 2022 Chestnut Review Prose Chapbook Prize, and her collection of short stories, *A New Day*, was a finalist for the 2021 St. Lawrence Book Award, and is forthcoming from She Writes Press in 2024. Her short story "Chances Are" appears in the Unleash Press *Conversations Anthology*. Other work has appeared in *Cleaver Magazine, Hippocampus Magazine, Jellyfish Review, Narrative Magazine* and elsewhere. Find her at suemell.com

I'm Just Telling You How It Is

On my sixty-first birthday, I'll go out for dinner with my brother, who'll have been at the rehab with my mom that afternoon while I continue cleaning and arranging things in preparation for her return home after a catastrophic fall.

Ordering cases of adult diapers, wipes, and the disposable under-pads that will protect her sheets and save me from constant laundering.

Returning yet another set of the drapes she'll need for warmth and privacy, but that, despite my careful study of online images and fabric content, have turned out to be too sheer—or simply too ugly—for the French doors between the drafty sunporch on this side of the house and the little-used dining room I'm making over into a first-floor bedroom.

I'm thinking sushi—something I've missed from my former non-caregiver life in San Francisco, where I wrote and indulged in too much TV and intermittently worked as a photo stylist to cover my rent. As a stylist, I specialize in soft goods: I'm the one who plumps the pillows and strews luxurious comforters across four-post beds, who makes colorful stacks of sheets and towels look perfect for home decor websites and catalogues.

And—despite its metal rails—I'm determined to have my mom's new hospital-style bed made cozy with soft new sheets and her familiar, freshly washed duvet. But the bed's delivery is a complicating factor.

According to the social worker, once the rehab doctor, the physical therapy department, and Medicare all sign off, the bed usually arrives the day before, the day of, or the day after the patient comes home. The day after? Where's she supposed to sleep? All the bedrooms are on the second floor and she can't make it up the fourteen wooden steps that nearly killed her when she tumbled down. We could move my brother's old twin downstairs for a night, but it's not something I relish adding to my to-do list.

"I'm just telling you how it is," the social worker says. I've often doubted her competence, but the exhaustion in her voice—and her slight departure from the usual party line—convinces me of the truth of this.

Eight more days, and then my life—like my mom's—will utterly change. My private retreat in the house I grew up in will come to a close, the future of living with her an uncertain enterprise. Cleaning and grocery shopping, meal planning and prep; bills, insurance claims, and follow-up appointments with doctors and physical therapists; refilling and administering her medications; keeping her spirits up and filling the ever-increasing gaps in her memory. Letting other stylists take up my hard-earned gigs and putting aside my San Francisco life to take care of hers.

How much more settled I would feel if I could make my mom's bed.

An Anthology

Carrie Lee South

Carrie Lee South is an MFA candidate at the University of Central Arkansas where she serves as the fiction editor for Arkana. Her work has appeared in *The Mid/South Anthology,* Opus Comics, *The Dread Machine, The Hunger*, and elsewhere. She keeps a small flock of parrots and is working on her first novel. Follow her @CarrieLeeSouth

Charades

Only after we've arrived do they tell us that we will be interviewed as a group. We glance at each other and shrug, because we might as well. We've already submitted our resumes, retyped the same information from those resumes into the internal hiring portal, and passed the first round of screening questions.

Why do you want this job?

What are your weaknesses?

If you were shrunk to the size of a pencil and put in a blender, how would you get out?

What was your most traumatic childhood experience?

Here we are, ill-fitting suits and fresh pantyhose and new haircuts. The receptionist smiles and ushers us to the conference room to meet our interviewers.

They are crocodiles. The panel of judges crouches behind the long table, thick, shining tails piled behind them. They spread their webbed claws, clicking against the mahogany as they rifle through a pile of papers. The leftmost reptile turns his snout sideways and looks me up and down. His marbled eye shutters closed as a membrane slides across to moisten it.

I turn to look at my co-interviewees, but they hardly show their nerves. The short girl is determined, jaw set, looking straight ahead. The boy with the slicked back hair clenches his fists. Only the girl wearing slacks returns my look. She licks her lips then faces forward again.

One of the crocodiles slides a piece of paper toward the receptionist. She clears her throat and reads from the paper: "Sell yourself in six words or less." We take turns.

"Creative independent with a growth mindset."

"Recent grad, perfectionist, ready to work."

"Happy to work nights and weekends."

I brace myself: "Confused, but excited to be here."

The crocodiles exhale loudly through their nostrils. It's hard to tell whether our answers are well-received, but their toothy jaws seem to be grinning cheerfully. They pass another sheet to the receptionist. She reads: "Pretend you are a seed. Without speaking, act as though you are bursting from the soil, sprouting, growing upwards, and blooming into a flower."

The other three immediately squat down and contort their bodies into round shapes. I follow suit. We push against the invisible dirt packed above us. The girl wearing slacks breaks through the crust first, her palms pressed together, then slowly opening like a seedling's first leaves. We wiggle upwards, slowly stretching our bodies into stems. Our hands open and close, leaves reaching to the sun of the fluorescent lighting, then finally blossom out from our smiling faces, arms stretched wide and waving like fluttering petals. We freeze.

One of the crocodiles emits a guttural sound. The receptionist nods and thanks us for our time. As she pulls out a spray bottle to mist her employers' scales, she miscalculates somehow. The closest crocodile thrashes and snaps its jaws closed around one of her legs. She lets out a gurgling scream while the crocodile spins into a death roll.

We ignore this and turn to the other three crocodiles. "Thank you so much for the opportunity, hope to hear from you soon." As we walk out into the bright sunlight of the day, shoulders slack with obvious relief, we shake each other's hands. "Good luck!"

An Anthology

Nancy Werking Poling

Nancy Werking Poling has worked as a public-school teacher, a textbook editor, and a writing tutor in a college learning center. She regrets having majored in sociology. Her published books include *While Earth Still Speaks*, a novel; *Before It Was Legal: a black-white marriage (1945-1987)*, nonfiction; *Had Eve Come First and Jonah Been a Woman*, a story collection; and *Out of the Pumpkin Shell*, a novel. Her short stories have appeared in numerous anthologies and small literary journals, most recently in the Chicago-themed anthology, *Open Heart Chicago*, and *Writing on the Edge*. Nancy lives and writes in the mountains of western North Carolina. nancypoling.com

Across a Stainless-Steel Counter

I grew up in the segregated South, in small-town Orlando before Disney. I drank from "White Only" water fountains, used "White Only" restrooms, and attended schools with white children. Daily I rode the city bus to and from school, seated while Black women and men stood at the back. I didn't notice.

After my senior year of high school, I worked as a waitress at a Holiday Inn restaurant. The cook was a Black man named Norman. Business kept us both busy most of our shift, but there were times when we'd finished preparation for the next surge of customers and had nothing to do.

Is my inquisitiveness about people a blessing or a curse? There have been times when I wanted to know about matters that were none of my business. But it was probably that curiosity along with Norman's kind-heartedness, that led to our discussions from opposite sides of a long stainless-steel counter.

Today I wonder what he thought about those times, for he was a mature man who had served in the military and had a family. I was a seventeen-year-old, with *deep* questions about The Meaning of Life. I don't recall specific conversations, only that they sometimes were about racial matters. I probably asked about his family and what he did when he wasn't working. No doubt I prattled on about my plans to attend college that fall, not considering his feelings about his children's opportunities.

Sometime over that summer a small group of my closest friends were sprawled on the living room floor of one of their homes. I started to tell about my conversations with Norman. Why I now had this remarkable new insight: some Black men possessed intellect and wisdom!

My friends teased me. Are you in love with Norman? Are you going to marry him? The possibility that I could be friends with a Black man was ridiculous. That I might marry a Black man even more ludicrous. The memory of that evening is stamped on my mind: my shock that they didn't understand. They didn't *want* to understand.

But I, for the first time in my young life, caught a glimpse of what racism was. I couldn't have put words to it, but I felt it.

I had come to see Norman and myself as equals. Of course, we weren't. He was a mature man, a father, who had seen much more of the world and of life. I was an immature girl.

But for me that summer job was a beginning. Thanks to Norman's willingness to take my inquisitiveness seriously, I had taken a step—small though it was—toward understanding racism in America.

An Anthology

Douglas Cole

Douglas Cole published six poetry collections and the novel The White Field, winner of the American Fiction Award. His work has been anthologized in *Best New Writing* (Hopewell Publications), *Bully Anthology* (Kentucky Stories Press) and *Coming Off The Line* (Main Street Rag Publishing).

He is a regular contributor to Mythaxis, providing essays and interviews with notable writers, artists and musicians such as Daniel Wallace (Big Fish), Darcy Steinke (Suicide Blond, Flash Count Diary) and Tim Reynolds (T3 and The Dave Matthews Band). He also writes a monthly piece called "Trading Fours" for Jerry Jazz Musician and was recently named the editor for "American Poetry" in Read Carpet, an international, multi-lingual journal from Columbia.

In addition to the American Fiction Award, he was awarded the Leslie Hunt Memorial prize in poetry, the Editors' Choice Award for fiction by *RiverSedge*, and has been nominated three time for a Pushcart and seven times for *Best of the Net*. He lives and teaches in Seattle, Washington. His website is douglastcole.com.

The Machine Shop at the End of the World

Then Larry moved me in to the storage and prep room where he handed me off to Tony, who was supposed to show me what to do next. He was a little guy with one of those thin scraggly beards that don't fully come in, like he didn't punch all the way through puberty. He was about my age, with long hair tied back in a ponytail. He wore a Doors shirt with Jim Morrison reaching out a warlock hand at me.

"Now what you do," he said, taking me over to a table covered by a beat-up sheet of tin and with a couple of large boxes full of little metal plates, "is you take one of these…" He took out a plate that was about the size of a book cover. Then he produced a jar of what looked like red play-dough. "You get yourself a hunk of this…" He pulled out a gob of the play-dough and rolled it between his fingers. "And roll it into a ball…and you…" The plate had holes of various sizes in it, and he worked the putty into the holes. "You've got to get it in here and make sure it fits all the way around the inside edge of the hole," he said, "so that no paint can get in. But you can't get any of it on the surface of the plate, here, you see? Ya got it?"

"I think so," I said.

"And you've got to fill every hole," he said. He spoke softly, working the play-dough into the holes of the plate with a delicate, jeweler's care. Sometimes his tongue would appear between his lips. And as he worked, his thin fingers flipped the plate around like spider legs wrapping up a fly.

"Get a plate," he said. "By the time you're done, you'll know how many holes it takes to fill the Albert's Hall."

I laughed. "Nice. All right, *John.*"

I took a plate from the box, a jar of the putty, and started working on my new task. It wasn't as easy as it looked, though, especially with my blistered hand still healing, the flesh on my palm buckling when I gripped the metal plates. Sometimes the putty wouldn't stick to the edge, and sometimes, after I had gotten nearly all of the holes filled, a putty disc would fall out, or I'd knock it out by accident, or my hands would sweat so bad from the dreamy oppressive swelter of heat in that room that the putty would smear on the surface of the plate.

"Ah! Tony," I said, laughing, "I don't think I'm doing too well here."

"Don't worry about it," he said, rotating the plate in his hand so fast and easy he barely seemed to touch it. "You'll get the hang of it."

He was done with about eight of the plates by the time I had barely finished two. But I kept at it. I felt determined to master this one task. And for a long time we didn't say anything to each other. We just worked while we listened to the radio that was sitting up on one of the metal shelves. It was set to a classic rock and roll station: Janis Joplin, The Beatles, The Stones, Van Morrison, Steely Dan, that sort of thing. And every once in a while I would hear Tony humming along with one of the songs.

Finally, I asked him, "So how long you been working here, Tony?"

"About four years," he said. "I've been here the longest."

"Really? And you've been doing this the whole time?"

"Yeah. Adam's curse. I do this, and I'm pretty much in charge of openings and closings, which just means opening the doors at dawn and closing them at sunset, although I like to say opening and closing because it sounds more important. So if someone asks me what I do, I say

I'm in charge of opening and closing the shop. Doesn't that sound good?" and he smiled ironically, pointing back to the wide, sliding doors.

"So you're the one in control of letting us in and out," I said.

"Yeah. You know, I've actually been here longer than Larry has."

"Yeah? Who was here before him?"

"His father. This weird guy named Hurd. He's the one who owns the place. Or he did own it. I think he might be dead, now."

"Ah."

"But, Larry doesn't know what the fuck he's doing."

I laughed.

"In fact, you watch. It's pretty funny. Larry does all the silk screening, right? You know, for instrument panels and that sort of thing. You have to use these stencils, and it's pretty delicate work, really. I mean, it's not that hard, either. But Larry thinks he's the only one here who can do it right. He thinks we're all a bunch of idiots. I used to do it, when his father ran the place, but whatever. But the problem is, and what Larry doesn't seem to understand after, I don't know, more than a year?, is that when it gets hot like this and you try to silk screen the panels---—well, you'll see. He's such a dumb fuck he doesn't know that you have to wait till it cools down. It's the paint—he always fucks it up. And then he gets all pissed off and starts cussing and screaming, total tantrum."

"__"

"Oh, you'll love it. Poor guy. I do feel sorry for him. And he didn't used to be this fat, but he's got diabetes or a heart condition or something, I'm not sure what, and they put him on some medication about six months ago, and he just bloated up overnight. It changed him. He was always a punk, but now he's a sick fat punk. I can't imagine he's got much time left."

"That doesn't sound right."

"Yeah, but you watch. The next time he does a silk screen. You watch. You'll get a kick out of it."

"All right."

And for the rest of the afternoon we worked in the dream heat fixing putty balls into metal plates, listening to the radio play songs like *Waitin' on a Friend* and *People are Strange*, Jim Morrison coming out of the radio and through Tony's chest with that hand reaching out and leveling on me a talismanic charge or a command or a final request to follow, I could never be sure what, while Tony hummed along with the music. Then the Byrds came on, singing *Eight Miles High.*

"I feel about eight miles low," I said, shaking my head, trying to rid myself of the writhing in my skull.

"Little too much afterburn, eh?"

"You know it," I said.

"In the sweat of thy face shalt thou find bliss," he said.

"I don't know about that."

The guitar rippled rapid-fire pulses, rising, higher and higher. "Pretty amazing guitar," I said.

"Roger McGuinn," Tony said. "He's definitely a genius. His real name was actually James Joseph McGuinn. For some reason, he changed it around the same time that he got into this Indonesian religion called Subud. Subud? Yeah, that's right." Tony didn't even look up from the metal plate he was working on but continued to rattle off facts. "He was heavily influenced by jazz and modeled this guitar solo on a John Coltrane song. He played, I believe it was, a Rickenbacker 12-string and had it worked up somehow to sound like a saxophone. And the song, this one, was actually banned because it was considered to be a drug song, but the band members all said that it was really about a plane flight to London, yeah right, and culture shock, or something like that. At first it was titled *Six Miles High*, but then Gene Clark thought 'eight' sounded better than 'six' and that it would be a good catchy tune since the Beatles had just recently come out with *Eight Days A Week*. Smart, eh?"

"You really know a lot about this song, don't you?" I said.

"Oh, sure, I love the Byrds. I love all music, really, but especially Rock music."

"Yeah? Tell me more. What else do you know?"

Again, without looking up from his work, and with his fingers working deftly, filling in the little holes with little bits of putty, he recited. "Let's see. This song came out on their album *Fifth Dimension*. David Crosby is also listed as one of the composers, as a matter of fact. Many consider the album to be one of their weaker efforts, interestingly enough even though this is one of their most popular original compositions, probably because, like Dylan, they were moving on from the folk sound. *5D*, as they were called, actually played a mix of folk and jazz from the very beginning. Oh, and they have this one spooky song called *I Come and Stand At Every Door* about a child burned in the bombing of Hiroshima whose spirit walks the earth in search of peace, based on a poem written by…Nazim Hikmet and…," he looked up, finding the thought, "translated by Pete Seeger. Yep. Pete Seeger."

"Wow!" I said. "How do you know all that?"

"I hear it on the radio sometimes. I read a lot of it on jacket covers, mostly. Some books, too. Johnny Rogan has a book out on the Byrds called *Timeless Flight*. I read that one. I read a lot of things. I read history, too, mostly about the times when these guys were playing. And I just remember a lot of things. My brain is weird that way. Like, let's see, when *Five D* came out, 1966, the US and Soviet Union both landed probes on the moon, same year; Mao's Red Guard started gearing up in China then, too; Johnson started bombing in North Vietnam after a break of about a month; they started selling those little disposable flash bulbs, I don't know, do you remember those? Let's see, what else: that guy Whitman shot those people down in Texas at the university, and that guy Speck killed those nurses in Chicago, a lot of violence that year; um, those two Boeing planes crashed, that was a big deal, and those floods hit Italy and everybody was crying about the art that got destroyed, not the people; FM started getting big around that time, and so did *Mission Impossible,* that was the big show; then, *Valley of the Dolls* and *In Cold Blood* both came out, and they were big; Liz Taylor won best actress for *Who's Afraid of Virginia Woolf?*; the Celtics won the NBA championships; the Orioles won the World Series; hey, and Billie Jean King, do you remember her? She won Wimbledon that year. They published a study that said monkeys deprived of social contact become emotionally impaired, duh—I could go on forever. I love history, really, as long as it pertains to the music. Some of it sticks, anyway, obviously. But if there's no connection to the music, I'm not interested. But you know, I usually find there is some connection to events in history and the songs these guys are writing, especially the classic rock period. That's my favorite. Although, I've begun to branch out because classical music influenced them and they influenced the music that came after them."

"Which comes first?" I asked. "The history or the music?"

Tony laughed. "I often wonder."

"You remember everything in pretty good detail, too," I said.

"Yeah. I remember everything I read. All of it. I can't not remember it, in fact."

"Why, Tony," I said, "you're a scholar."

He lifted up a metal plate full of putty and waved it at me. "Yeah, right. I never made it past the tenth grade."

***

Larry came in, then, towards the end of the day. He went right past us without saying a word, and Tony grinned and said in a low voice so that Larry couldn't hear him, "here we go. Keep your eyes open. Show's about to start."

I glanced over at Larry who was arranging a set of black panels for silk screening. He was lining them up in a rack next to the silk screen and arranging canisters of paint and paddles.

"Control panels," Tony whispered. "They come with these special stencils and have to be aligned very precisely, get it? And not only do you have to line them up properly, but they have to have a sharp line so that they're readable, but in this heat, the paint's going to run." Larry took his time, carefully aligning the stencils, fixing the clamps, setting up his paint. "He doesn't even realize it's way too hot," Tony said. Then, Larry pooled the paint along one edge, wiped it across the stencil with the bat, pulled back the stencil and looked at it.

"Mother fuck!" he shouted.

Tony shot me a glance, raised one eyebrow and grinned. "It's just starting. It gets better."

Larry went through the process again with another plate and pulled the stencil back and looked at it and said, "Mother fuck!" only louder and more shrill this time. He wiped the two plates down, stripped them with a rag soaked in solvent and then set them aside to dry and laid down another plate and tried again. When he pulled back the stencil and looked at what he had done, he screamed even louder, "Mother fuck! Cock sucker!" And he held the plate up over his head like he wanted to throw it through someone's skull, his hands shaking with rage. Then he put it down, wiped it clean, and took one of the previously cleaned plates that had now dried. He started again. Only now he was more careless, throwing down the plate, slapping on the stencil, slopping on the paint hopelessly. And when he failed for the fourth time, he screamed again, "Ahhhh you fucker, fucker, fucker!" swinging his arms and kicking but not actually hitting anything, his fury thrown into the empty air, his rage going nowhere.

Tony shook his head. "I've seen it a million times."

Adam J. Galanski

Adam J Galanski's writing has appeared in *BULL*, *Contraposition*, *Crack the Spine*, *The Manilla Envelope*, and more. His novella, *The Toughest Girl in Town* is forthcoming in the Running Wild Press Novella Anthology #6. His novel, *Szarotka*, is the winner of the 2022 Buffalo Books Prize in Fiction and will be published by American Buffalo Books/Kansas State University Press in Summer 2024. Adam maintains a website at ajgart.net. He lives in Chicago.

Night at the Roach Palace

"I wasn't always a working stiff…"

Saul had his chihuahua slung over his shoulders like a lamb. "You know," he said, "When I was a kid in Mexico, we used to torture dogs like this. Street dogs. We'd break their legs, shoot them with pellets, cut them up… I didn't care. But when I saw Pancho, I knew I couldn't be like that anymore." His gray hair was half combed back in grease from the heat of the kitchen stove. The other half dangled lazily off the side of his head. I didn't know it at the time but this would be the last I ever saw of him.

Ravenswood Avenue was silent, save the occasional car speeding by. The castle turret gates of Chicago's Rosehill Cemetery loomed in the distance under a sunset fading from an autumn orange into a purple bruise. I was carrying boxes of beer to Fireside's back cooler, where he stood at the delivery gate, puffing a joint in his lips.

"You're crazy man…"

"This place is crazy," He nodded towards a hefty brown cockroach, crawling down the phone counter by the open alley door. "You know, I brought them here."

"They're everywhere."

"Think I give a shit man? I got 'em back home. Won't be here much longer anyway. Ruben's brought me back three times," he shook three fingers at me, "Every time I hate it more. Just getting back at Larry before I go."

If revenge was what he desired, it was a job well done. We were serving up cockroaches by the platter. They lurked in every crevice of the kitchen. The place was overrun. If you shook the pizza boxes above the oven, dozens of the fuckers would scatter across the walls. We were hand delivering pests all the way across Andersonville, Edgewater, Uptown, and Rogers Park.

"Asian and German roaches, big and small. A major infestation" my manager, Asher, said, sipping a pale ale from a perpetually replenished rocks glass, amidst the bleak stretch of hours of the graveyard shift. When he finished the glass he walked to the taps and pulled another. To any passing customer it looked like he was merely having a taste.

Our barroom was open to four AM. Five AM on Saturdays. The kitchen was open until three AM. I started at ten PM, if not earlier, on nights I had to stock deliveries and take inventory. But for the roaches there was no better or worse time of day. The infestation didn't cease for an enjoyable brunch. And they brazenly crawled across the bar top at the dinner rushes. Our more loyal regulars turned blind eyes in sympathy to the situation. They casually lifted their plates to let the insects pass before signaling a waiter with a low wave of the hand.

 I had them crawl out of my salads on break. A few times I ladled them out of our ranch dressing dish in the kitchen expo. Once they even scampered from the recesses of my buffalo wings when enjoying a drink on my day off. "Extra protein," a coworker assured me. I turned and raised my eyebrows to him. He pushed his glasses back up the bridge of his nose. The skin on his face was tight and smug in a shit-eating grin.

The basement of the restaurant was cramped and unfinished. The low ceiling forced me to hunch over as I lugged around half barrel kegs in the flickering of the dim tungsten lights. At the turn of the stairs there came a point where the walls did not completely connect. Within that gap a whole civilization, or better yet, a parallel universe of cockroaches crawled and festered like twisted gears of Hell's creation.

I always made sure to look up. They'd fall off the ceiling into my hair, crawl on my neck, get in my clothes. When changing Co2 tanks, I swiped them away with thwacks of my wrench, holding the tubing in my other hand, trying not to drop the o-ring gasket in the dark. Mystery liquid would drip down into my hair from the moaning pipes, leaking just above my head.

"That better not be the septic…"

I'd often sit in the rotting basement toilet stall, observing the Mexican cook's graffiti of a blunt and the words, "Mota is good." The rubber heel of my Doc Martin boots splattered any cockroach that drew too close. We couldn't even shit in peace. And somehow it was still a taboo subject among the employees. especially with Larry, the owner, around.

An old customer had dubbed Fireside, "The Diarrhea Palace" thanks to the instant effects of our brand of comfort food. But I called it "The Roach Palace". It was a more fitting nickname those days. And a paid off health inspector did wonders to keep it that way.

***

Saul had his dog on the ground. He connected the leash to its collar and unlocked his bicycle to head back to Albany Park. I took my dolly stacked with Miller Lite cases and carted them out past the empty back patio. Strings of white lights glowed above the tables, rocking in the cool of the breeze. In the walk-in fridge I cursed and thrashed wet boxes of expired beer and old moldy six packs across the sunken shelves.

Grit coated bottles fell out of the blown-out undersides of Budweiser cardboard boxes, halfheartedly spinning to a stop. Stale beer sputtered like a faucet from under the caps out onto the floor. I grumbled and brushed the sticky drip of the ceiling fan condensation off the edge my brow ridge. Muffled chirps sounded out with the struggle of feathers. I paused to glance through the open door, where the frost of the AC unit bellowed into a mist in its collision with the evening's heat.

A young robin was stuck on its back, its wings outstretched in a rectangular glue trap. The city had demolished the building next door, leaving us to inherit the burden of the lot's rodent inhabitants. Larry had lined traps on the outskirts of the property, and anywhere there was beer or food. Now instead of a disease ridden city rat, there was a delicate, charming little bird glued there to the last starved moments of its transient life. It was like Jesus on the crucifix. And God gave me a spear.

In the corner of the cooler was a sledgehammer that belonged to the building's handyman. I brandished it with both hands above my head ready to drive the bird in like a steel railroad spike. The bird quivered, engaging me with desperate eyes, as if to barter for salvation. It didn't know that its death would be worse without me. There would be no ripping it from the trap without tearing apart its wings and torso. Still I hesitated, reaching into my back pocket to pull out my cloth bar towel, and lay it over the robin's body.

"I hope you fly to heaven," I whispered. Its helpless chirps rose to a crescendo. In another moment I had raised the hammer and dropped it down on the glue trap with an uncomfortable thud. It unfolded with the anticipation of a carnival game made to rate your strength. In the end all it proved was I still had a heart left inside my chest.

 I stared at the soiled rag, hands gripping the sledgehammer, trying to make some sort of peace. My chest swelled in and out, audibly breathing. Then I leaned the tool against the cooler, grabbed the empty dolly, and casually rolled it back inside to stock more beer. Looking over my shoulder I shuddered at the sight of the bloody bar towel waiting there like an abandoned child, rose red and sheet white in the black of the endless night. The frantic whistles were nothing but an old song now, percussively crooning in the back of my mind.

***

Jimmy Moran was in the barroom. His face was as red as his hair. He was what we called a "career alcoholic". It wasn't uncommon. Jimmy Moran prided himself on his Irish heritage. "Irish Jimmy" as he would introduce himself to strangers. The neighborhood kids were hogging the jukebox, blasting trap music. Jimmy shouted at me over their selections. I was busy washing glassware. My hands bobbed up and down in the unchanged murky water of our warm sinks. My back was hunched crooked, my cap pointing down over my eyes.

"Me and the kiddos gonna take the van up to Wisconsin for the weekend. We got a camping spot up there. We go fishing, we grill. I got fucking Jager on tap! Jager on tap!" The song changed, "What's this shit? I wanna hear rock and roll!" Jimmy started getting into it with the local kids. He threw a barrage of dollar bills in the jukebox. "I'm gonna show you some real music," he assured. They were amused by him.

"You mad bro?" one laughed.

"Of course I'm mad!" Jimmy roared, "I got the curse of the Irishman- the angry inch!" He did another few shots of Jager, paid his tab, then peeled out in his ramshackle cargo van, speeding blindly down the narrow lanes of Ravenswood Avenue. Irish Jimmy had a DUI and wasn't supposed to be driving. But I couldn't stop him. I didn't care to either. "Fuckin' Jager on tap!" his voice echoed in my head. I smiled.

***

At last call I was asked to phone a cab for an old man whose wife was dying of cancer at Thorek Memorial Hospital. He had been coming to the bar every day for two weeks straight while she received her final treatment. And he made a habit of hovering over the young ladies in the room until his unwarranted touches and attempted kisses repulsed them into paying their bills. After each rejection he muttered bitter phrases in Urdu that only the cab drivers in the corner could decipher.

I was always reluctant to call a cab. The cab companies hated us. Over fifty percent of our customers who requested a ride ended up walking off into the night in a drunken stupor, or passing out slumped over in broken glass by the cemetery gates. Not to mention throughout the night all the drunks fiddled around on their smart phones in a line down the counter, acting as if they couldn't complete the task themselves.

Some latin gang bangers popped in to get four, twenty four packs of Modelo to go, flashing loose wads of cash from their pockets. Asher, whose eyes were crossed behind his glasses, started pouring the boys a line of shots before falling into a rail of well bottles, spilling Jameson all over the floor-mats. "Opa!"a lady yelled from the doorway. Asher wheezed with laughter.

When I came back from the cooler with their order, Asher was propped against the brass taps, filling his rocks glass with a pale ale. It erupted with a thick head of white foam which bubbled over onto the stomach of his blue collared shirt. I punched in the one phone number I knew off the top of my head, listening to the 90's knockoff R&B recordings for a good five minutes, while Flash Cab kept me on hold in hopes that they wouldn't have to take my business.

"Where you going? They wanna know," I asked the guy, finally getting through to a human. One of the cab drivers translated for him, then translated his answer back to me.

"Heart of Chicago Motel, Alex. Peterson and Ridge."

"Got it."

"Sorry, what was the passenger's destination?" the operator repeated.

"Yes, he says he's going to 63rd and Halsted…" I nodded and waved to the old man. He smiled and put his thumb in the air, having no idea he was taking a ride to the heart of Englewood on Chicago's South Side.

"Alright! Get out! I gotta clean up! We have a snuff film to shoot here in the next half hour!" A few customers chuckled at my joke. Most weren't even listening.

"I wanna see a snuff film!" one man retorted.

"Ok, I'll pencil you in! C'mon I gotta close…" He blew a fart at me with his lips and waved his hands in dismissal.

With palms clutching their guts, the wet brained scoundrels carried their damaged livers past the clouds of drain flies, in a pitiful shuffle out the door, yapping over each other's vapid stories that had been repeated, reshaped, and proved a lie daily over the course of an entire lifetime, punching in and out like clockwork at the stations of their bow-legged stools.

***

By 5:30 AM, I had finished up. There was a cool mist spreading low above the cemetery and METRA train tracks across the street. Asher offered me a ride home in his Cadillac but it was nice enough that I walked.

The birds of the cracking dawn sang in a chorus from the shadows. Planes hummed above, red and yellow lights blinking through the woolly clouds. They would soon be touching down at O'hare.

On Work

Two coyotes lurked along the sloped train tracks running parallel with the shaded trees of Ravenswood Avenue. They trailed me from a distance watching my body at every step. It was more curious than threatening.

A commuter sped by. I turned the corner and the coyotes were gone. A mile later, on Winthrop and Balmoral, I ran up the groaning backstairs to my third-floor apartment. The kitchen light was left on for me.

There was a distant rumble and chiming bell of the red line train reaching the Berwyn stop behind my building. A vagrant walked a cheap bicycle through the alley below with a basket filled with trash attached to the front. Bags of cans and dirty clothes hung off the sides. I had seen him before, drinking forty ounces with his friends under the tracks. We locked eyes.

"My brother Ted died in that apartment, 20 years ago!" He yelled. His fist was up in the air. He had told me this before. The man started to say more, but the El train pulled through and drowned out his words. I went inside to my cats, my wife and the comfort of our bed, to sleep.

An Anthology